"When change affects an organization, the leaders of the organization—from the top executive to line supervisors—need to demonstrate leadership skills as never before. The role of the manager becomes critical in leading teams and employees through the change process so that the organization can implement new ideas, and maintain its customers while retaining and engaging talented employees."

"Significant organizational change has a powerful impact on people. Change creates a tension between the past and the future, between stability and the unknown. Despite business rationale, logic, creativity, planning, and strategies associated with change, this tension comes down to people doing different things in different ways. Asking people to change behavior on behalf of organizational goals creates an automatic emotional reaction."

"Personally refocusing asks the manager to examine personal feelings, motives, and assumptions about change. It is the place to start understanding how to be a change leader."

Managing in Times of Change

✔ 24 Lessons for Leading Individuals and Teams through Change

MICHAEL D. MAGINN

McGRAW-HILL

New York Chicago San Francisco Lisbon
London Madrid Mexico City Milan New Delhi
San Juan Seoul Singapore Sydney Toronto

1 2 3 4 5 6 7 8 9 0 DOC/DOC 0 9 8 7 6

ISBN-13: 978-0-07-148436-7
ISBN-10:   0-07-148436-1

Contents

Managing in Times of Change

☑ Managing in times of change

A basic fact of business life is that an organization either changes or withers away. Look at the power-house companies in today's world. Where were they 10 or 20 years ago? Have they grown, changed business models, or emerged from nowhere? What's happened to some of the brand names with which you grew up? Which established airlines, banks, car companies, or heavy manufacturing companies have struggled to match lower-cost, more efficient competitors? It's either nimbly and creatively adapt with new products, processes, and business ideas or go into marketplace decline.

Whether a company is on the upside of the growth curve or fighting to survive, one thing is common: the people working within those organizations are experiencing change in a very personal way. Employees have to stop what they have been doing and work in different ways with different—or fewer—team members. They may have to work away from home more frequently or move to another facility in a strange, new city. They have to work with new technologies that require new skills, say new things to customers, meet with each other more or less frequently, or do more with less.

When people face these kinds of dramatic changes in the way they live and work, the reaction can be negative and unproductive. What had been predictable and stable at work is now replaced by confusion, vagueness, and uncertainty.

When change affects an organization, the leaders of the organization—from the top executive to line supervisors—need to demonstrate leadership skills as never before. The manager becomes critical in leading teams and employees through the change process so that the organization can implement new ideas and maintain its customers while retaining and engaging talented employees.

The managers of an organization provide the bridge from the old way of doing things to new work practices. Paradoxically, these managers are also employees who experience the same reactions as everyone else. How can a leader lead when he or she may be uncertain and uncomfortable about the future?

There are productive behaviors that a manager can learn to cope with change and to help others through. These behaviors can be clustered into three major themes:

Personally refocus for managers. The first step in helping others implement change is to help yourself. Managers need to understand how they are personally reacting and how change is affecting them. Once they understand their reaction, they can adapt to their role.

Lead the team through. A work group needs strong leadership to provide direction, a degree of clarity, and sense of progress when there aren't clear answers to questions and rumors begin to fly. The manager needs to help the team adapt to and cope with newness.

Show a path to individuals. Individuals react to change in different ways. Until a change has taken root within a work group, some individuals may need extra coaching and advice on how to cope. The manager needs to sit with employees with strong, unproductive reactions to change to instill a firm, optimistic picture of the future.

"I was always for change until it happened to me."

—Midlevel financial services manager

PERSONALLY REFOCUSING FOR MANAGERS: Understand how change affects you

Significant organizational change has a powerful impact on people. Change creates a tension between the past and the future, between stability and the unknown. Despite business rationale, logic, creativity, planning, and strategies associated with change, this tension comes down to people doing different things in different ways. Asking people to change behavior on behalf of organizational goals creates an automatic emotional reaction.

Managers are certainly not immune from this response. Even managers responsible for implementing change within an organization can subtly undermine that change through the words they use to describe it and what they do to support it.

To be a successful leader of change, a manager has to first understand the dynamics of change and the ways uncertainty affects them and others. The old way has to be mourned; the new way has to be understood. The change leader has to recognize how ambiguity can be used to adapt to changes, how improvisation forces work units to make the best of their situations, and how change ratchets up the need for clear, crisp communications.

Most important of all, the change leader has to see himself or herself as the role model toward whom all team members look for cues and clues about how they should respond to the changing situation.

Personally refocusing asks the manager to examine his or her individual feelings, motives, and assumptions about change. It is the place to start understanding how to be a change leader.

"I can't change the direction of the wind. But I can adjust my sails."

—Anonymous

☐ Stop at the headlines

☑ Understand the "from–to"

Organizational change can be defined in a simple way. Change happens when the organization is moved from the status quo to something different. "From-to" is the change. "We are going *from* being individual cost centers to regional profit centers." "Our managers are transitioning *from* being administrators *to* revenue managers." "We are moving *from* being a high-service, high-cost provider *to* being the low-cost market leader."

While this strategic description of change is a useful start, it doesn't help a work unit manager to really understand what will happen to him or the members of the team at the grass roots level.

A critical part of personal refocusing is actually being able to trace what the from-to will be in a work unit. Once the manager understands that impact, he or she will be better able to explain it to the team.

The process of understanding the from-to is answering a series of questions about the organization. Bear in mind, you may not be able to answer all of these items initially. That's what makes for ambiguity, a key by-product of the change experience.

Start with the mission: Why is the organization here in the first place? Has that objective changed? What about those you serve? Are your customers different? Most likely, your approach or strategy will be different. What you do to serve your customers may be shifting from, say, a centralized focus to a regional orientation where decisions about customers are made in the field instead of the home office.

How about how success is measured? Are old standards being replaced by new standards? Are different kinds of measures now in place that seem unfamiliar or even difficult to grasp, such as customer loyalty? Changes in measurements and standards can often be a source of anxiety from employees because compensation is most likely tied to these new success indicators.

What about how work actually gets done? Are there new processes to install and implement? Will new or fewer people be asked to do the work? Will the work unit gain or lose tools and resources? Will the team be managed differently? What will be the role of the managers in the new from-to environment? Will they have to become player-coaches, maintaining their own personal individual accounts or contributor workload, or will they have to give up their individual work entirely and manage all the time?

How will the work unit adapt? On what will the team have to focus, or of what will it need to do more or less? What will stay the same?

When a manager can answer these questions as completely as possible, the extent and impact of the from-to change will become clearer.

Analyze what is happening. Take a step back and think through the implications of the change. When thinking about different aspects of work, keep asking yourself, "How will this be affected?"

Isolate the big impacts. Every change has at least one—usually more—major implications for how things operate. Locate what those are.

Use your imagination. The impact of many of these changes is unforeseen at the planning stage. Keep your mind open to what might happen and how people might feel.

"It isn't the changes that kill you; it's the transitions."

—**William Bridges**

LEARN

UNLEARN

RELEARN

☑ Choose a productive response

Change happens to us every day. We miss our usual train to work, the highway has a detour, the weather is colder or hotter than we thought, we have a new e-mail system, we have to submit time sheets, we are asked to sign up for meeting room reservations, we have to change our schedule because someone can't make a meeting. Countless little events make our days different from one another. Some of these force us to change or stop our usual behavior, causing irritation and grumbling. "Why should we make meeting room reservations now? We never had to before." Others are just absorbed into our routine. By the second day, the road detour has become familiar, we find we can do neat things with the new e-mail system, and so life goes on. We learn, we adapt, we continue with what was once unfamiliar.

On the other hand, there are some changes that come along, usually once in a while or once in a career, that cause big discomfort and major stress. Our company has merged with another; we are not sure who will be asked to continue working. We have a new manager who is more demanding. Our work group has been asked to move out of town. A favorite work colleague, friend, and mentor has retired, and no one is replacing her. You have to do your job and part of someone else's job. The compensation system has been changed.

One way to react to this kind of change is to respond unproductively. Typically, that response is a natural defensive reaction and not usually made on purpose. Withdraw into a private world and take caution in what you say and to whom you say it. Play the disenchanted employee ("Things were better back when . . ."); refuse to make decisions until information is totally complete and accurate; overreact or feel powerless ("There's nothing I can do about that").

Yet, there is a more productive way to react to change. Acknowledge your loss, yet make a conscious decision to cope and remain positive and productive. The merger situation may result in greater opportunities, or you may meet interesting colleagues and learn more about your profession. Show creativity in muddling through situations that aren't completely clear; test your experience and intuition by making decisions as best you can.

12

Pressing on the positive switch is an important first step for a manager responsible for getting results from people. Consider these ideas:

Recognize your unproductive response. If you find yourself resisting the change, or seeing only the negative aspects of it, reflect on how you are feeling about what has happened and what will happen. Unproductive reactions include withdrawal, denial, and overreacting.

Cope. To cope means to make the best of your situation. Recognize the difficulties you are facing and decide to deal with them in a positive way.

Be yourself. Change is going to happen regardless of what you do. Let go of the past and get ready to move on. This adjustment isn't always easy, but it is necessary.

"The illiterate of the 21st century will not be those who cannot read and write, but those who cannot learn, unlearn, and relearn."
—Alvin Toffler

☐ ~~Emphasize the obstacles~~

☑ Seek the opportunity

Here is an interesting exercise: think of a change that is affecting your organization or team. From the *organization's* point of view, identify what the positive as well as negative consequences of that change will be. Now, from your *individual* perspective, list what you feel are the positive and negative outcomes. Review your responses.

Chances are the list of negative outcomes for you is as long as the list of positive outcomes for your organization. Typically, many people tend to see organizational change as first and foremost benefiting the organization, not the people who work there. For example, if the organization is moving its headquarters to a suburban location from a downtown area, the business positives include lower expenses, expandable space, better communication among departments that will now be in one location, tax benefits, and so on. Employees, however, may view this impending move as nothing but bad news: they may have a longer commute, a need to buy a car, more time away from family, uninteresting lunch options, and a change in the "feel" of the company. Yet, if you think about it, the new location will have more room, better lighting and furniture, more exposure to others in the company, a gym, and outdoor tables for meetings or lunch. The personal opportunity is to work together more effectively, get some exercise, and have a better total work experience.

The point is that we tend to see personal negatives before we see the positives in a change situation. When it comes to personal refocusing, a manager needs to look objectively at the change situation to determine what positives there are either actually or potentially for him- or herself. The key is to look beyond your first reaction.

Where is the opportunity? Imagine your organization is moving to a team concept in dealing with clients. Instead of individual specialists calling on a client, the individual specialists have become a coordinated team, calling on clients in a systematic way, presenting integrated solutions that solve a number of client problems rather than one or two at a time. While that approach initially looks as if you are no longer an individual "star" in the eyes of the client, the opportunity is to creatively work with other professionals, develop innovative approaches, and learn how other professionals think.

If your new manager is asking your team to take on new tasks, the opportunity is to get your team to discuss how it can work more effectively, an effort and challenge you can lead. If your group is being merged with another group, the opportunity is to create a seamless transition so that details, time, and expenses are not lost. If the group has new government regulations to implement, the opportunity is to train and motivate the team to make it happen.

Find the rainbow. Think carefully about where the opportunity might be in the change situation. Where can you shine? What can you learn? What impact can you make?

Banish negative thinking. Don't let obstacles appear so large that they stop you from seeing the opportunity that change represents. If you find yourself dwelling on the negatives, ask yourself why, and switch your perspective.

Look for the critical success factor. Any change is going to involve something special—coordination, motivation, teamwork, technical skill, leadership. Put yourself in a position to deliver what is needed.

"Opportunity is missed by most people because it comes dressed in overalls and looks like work."
—Thomas Edison

☐ ~~Go it alone~~

☑ **Gather your assets and resources**

It's clear that managing change in a work unit is a challenge. Many managers feel as if they are pushing change and dragging team members along to a new way of doing business, especially when the change is dramatic, such as taking on additional tasks, working with new partners, or changing work hours.

As part of the personal refocusing process, the wise manager needs to identify the tools and resources available to help him or her succeed. Without taking inventory of these assets, the manager can feel isolated when working through change.

What are these tools and resources? The manager's manager is probably the most important one. The "boss" has links to higher levels of the organization where different types of decisions are made and where information begins its downhill flow. The manager's manager can be a skill coach, a source of answers as well as a sounding board for ideas before they are implemented in the work unit.

A manager's personal network within an organization is also a vital resource. These are relationships outside formal reporting structures. The people in a personal network are colleagues, former managers, mentors, and friends who can be counted on for help, information, and ideas. A manager can also use this back-door, informal network to get things done. For example, if a manager feels a newly merged work unit needs a special brand of team building activity, he or she can access network friends who can recommend or even provide a training session.

A more tangible resource is training or reorientation programs. Most big changes in a company are supported by a variety of communications efforts—such as town meetings or frequently published newsletters and updates. Some change programs include teaching employees new skills to work in the changed environment. A company that is moving to a sales orientation, for example, will train engineers and technicians in customer service skills. A manager needs to understand what the organization is providing, what the purposes of these different elements are, and how he or she can take advantage of them.

Finally, an often-overlooked resource is the rationale for the change itself. A manager has to be able to understand and clearly and convincingly articulate the driving vision of the change and the opportunities it represents. This goal can help the team accept what is happening and why. "We are downsizing so we can focus on what we do best for the customer. Everyone is going to have a lot more experience in solving customer problems." "We are merging with a larger company so that we can gain technological resources and marketing strength that will widely distribute our products to new markets." The big picture sets the context for why individuals will be asked to do new and different things.

Stay in touch with your manager. He or she can often be the source of the latest news and information as well as a gateway to other parts of the organization.

Activate your network. Getting things done and finding out information informally may be more efficient. Keep in touch with old friends and acquaintances.

Support the corporate program. Communications, training, structured meetings, and presentations are your tools to use. Understand them and use them to help yourself.

"Become a student of change. It is the only thing that will remain constant."
—Anthony J. D'Angelo

☑ Forge personal goals

Change and opportunity go hand in hand. When work shifts and jobs change, there is a need for leadership, influence, technical understanding, and skilled communications. If you are a manager or member of a team, this is an opportunity to personally grow, develop new skills, and expertly apply established ones. Change can be a time for you to shine. Your task is to define what outcomes you personally want.

Let's say your work group is being asked to incorporate new measurements reflecting effectiveness in developing employees. So, in addition to the usual performance measures, there are new ones: How many new employees are certified in certain skill areas? How long did it take them to reach proficiency? What is their current level of performance compared to more experienced employees? These are fuzzy and ambiguous measurements at best; your job is to make it happen.

While there is a lot for a manager to do to get these measures installed, consider what a manager might personally take away from this situation:

The manager has a chance to position the reason for this change so that, while there is some initial resistance, team members come to understand the value in the numbers.

The manager can also be seen as the person who thoughtfully creates a consensus among the team members about how to take these measurements and document them.

The manager can use this change to inform and persuade senior management how to best implement these changes in other parts of the organization.

The manager can earn a reputation as a problem solver and conflict resolver, the person people go to when they have problems in adjusting to the changed environment.

These outcomes represent personal goals the manager can achieve in this experience. If the manager can consciously set these personal goals before the change process takes hold, the whole experience can be much more beneficial and rewarding.

Part of the personal refocus process is for the manager to form these specific personal goals that answer the question, "What do you want to get out of this?" Setting positive goals is a useful technique to help the manager shift from the natural, unproductive responses to actively engaging in the change.

Identify personal skill improvement areas. What skills do you need to improve? What skills have you had difficulty in performing in the past? Where do you need more practice? Look at implementing change and managing the team in changing times as a laboratory for your personal improvement.

Be bold; have courage. Change situations need champions, managers who go the extra distance to embrace what is new. Make yourself into a change champion; earn a reputation for effective change management.

Pick success indicators up front. Decide how you can tell you are achieving your goals. What will people be seeing or experiencing when they interact with you? Document both your goals and success indicators.

"The Chinese use two brush strokes to write the word 'crisis.' One brush stroke stands for danger; the other for opportunity. In a crisis, be aware of the danger—but recognize the opportunity."
—Richard Nixon

☐ ~~Do as I say~~

☑ Walk the talk

How would you feel about this? A manager explains that because of the changes the organization is facing, communications are a priority. Later, the manager can't be located when he or she is needed. How about the manager who believes in discussing reactions to the new compensation system "openly and honestly" but puts down negative comments from the team when they come up? Or, how about the manager who says that the new relationship management program's idea of sharing client information is a great idea, but his own client data is the last and least complete to be compiled? What does that do to support the changes?

"Walk the talk" is a basic leadership concept. When managers are trying to lead change in their organizations, they become beacons of attention. Their personal behavior becomes a model for others. When managers engage in new behaviors that are driven by changes, their entire team is watching.

What are they watching for? They are observing not only if you are doing what you say has to be done but also what your attitude is about doing it. They are asking with their eyes: "You are asking us to change. Are you changing, too?"

A manager moved with her team to a distribution center in a new city. She had advised the team to seek new connections in the community. Within weeks, that manager had personally joined local clubs, volunteered at charity organizations, represented the company at community business meetings, and staged parties where representatives from local civic and charity organizations met the staff. That manager was experiencing the dislocation of moving to a new city like everyone else. But she stepped up to her own advice—get involved with the community—and the transition was easier.

Another manager stated that frequent, early morning meetings were critical to the success of communications during a major change. Not only was that manager the first one present, he also provided breakfast and made the coffee.

Managers of work groups are the engines of change within organizations. If the manager walks the talk, keeps behavior consistent with messages, keeps commitments and promises, and demonstrates some energy and enthusiasm about what is happening, then team members will feel they can take the next step of commitment.

Watch your behavior. Managers are in the sights of all team members during change situations. Be careful what you say and do; it might inadvertently undermine the change message.

Show some enthusiasm and energy. Commitment comes through to others by words and deeds. Don't be shy about becoming a cheerleader for the change process.

Be the first; take on the most. Show up early for meetings, do more than others, and keep talking up the benefits of change. Make a decision that you are going to personify the change.

"The way to get started is to quit talking and begin doing."

—Walt Disney

☐ Wait for perfect clarity

☑ Make friends with ambiguity

Imagine that your company is merging with another organization. The announcement has just been made; however, the actual combination of work forces and systems will not begin for six months. You and your team are in the midst of a series of projects that are designed to streamline the way in which customer orders are processed. Should the projects continue? If so, should they have the same scope and budget as they did initially? Should the project teams remain assigned to these projects?

Or, what about this situation in which you manage a newly formed group of customer coordinators? The coordinator's role is either to solve customer problems directly or to hand them off to experts within the company. It is becoming clear that the distinction between which tasks are handled directly and which are handed off is blurred.

The risk of answering questions incorrectly or inconsistently can affect customer relations; passing too many problems to experts creates the impression that your group is nothing but glorified telephone operators. How can you deal with the gray areas?

Ambiguity is part of the change process. Ambiguity stems from lack of information about the future, vague guidelines, role confusion, overlapping responsibilities, unfinished plans, unanticipated consequences, and unclear decision-making processes. The good news is that ambiguity is normal and should be expected. Managers have to recognize that uncertainty comes with newness and change. Part of the personal refocusing process is to adapt to what can be uncomfortable and frustrating.

The unproductive responses to ambiguous situations are to wait for perfection or to withdraw. "I don't have enough information yet to make a decision." "The system doesn't work yet." "It's not my job." A more productive response to ambiguity is to recognize there are no perfect answers and to do the best you can under the circumstances. That means making decisions that might possibly turn out to be less than optimal or wrong.

This is called "muddling through" and requires ingenuity, creativity, and a strong feeling for what makes sense in your company and for your customers. Making decisions like this can feel like a "seat-of-the-pants" approach, improvised and instinctive. Many managers will find this process exhilarating. To others, it can be intimidating. The point is that work has to go on despite ambiguity—decisions have to be made, customers served, and processes improved. In time, ambiguity, vagueness, and gray areas may be better defined. But in changing times, managers have to get used to living with it.

Make decisions with the customer in mind. Your decisions in ambiguous situations can't be too far from wrong if you focus on what is best for your customers.

Don't be blocked by ambiguity. Recognize that there are many gray areas in changing times. Step up and be decisive when you can.

Collaborate with your colleagues. Make the most out of an ambiguous situation by getting colleagues and coworkers involved. You may find you can bring clarity and definition by talking things through.

"Uncertainty will always be part of the taking charge process."
—Harold Geneen

LEAD THE TEAM THROUGH:
How adaptable is your team?

The only systems that tend to stand the test of time are the adaptable ones. The ones your team works with are no exception.

The organization is changing because it needs to adapt to external pressures from competition, the workforce, and the marketplace. Those new changes trickle down to the work unit.

When change hits the work unit, it needs to adapt. The manager has a new role: change leader. He or she has to lead the adaptation process—a journey that can be confusing, complex, and complicated. The work unit faces new processes and procedures, new measures and means of controlling information. Technology may provide a substitute for familiar relationships with people. Teams face challenges with learning new responsibilities, dealing with changing authority or a different organizational structure, or adjusting to new or fewer people on board.

Regardless of the changing situation, the change leader has to take the team through the labyrinth of new relationships and processes while still meeting goals. The work unit manager has to communicate the organization's vision and make it meaningful.

When clarity breaks down, the manager has to help the team rediscover it. When rumors threaten progress, the manager has to squash them and teach the team how to deal with them. The change leader has to cheer progress, hold the line on standards, and generally get the work done.

Leading the team through describes how to manage the team in times of change.

"Adapt or perish, now as ever, is nature's inexorable imperative."

—H. G. Wells

☐ Get lost in the fog of change

☑ Paint a picture of what is happening

The manager of a team has a unique perspective. He or she has a wider view of the organization than team members have. The manager also is closer to information from higher levels in the organization. This extensive vantage point plays a critical role in changing times.

For example, at the top of the organization, the senior executive is responsible for describing his or her vision of what the company will become as a result of change. Whether it's a merger or reorganization, a shift to a new business model, major strategic innovation, or even a downsizing, the senior people need to express the new state that will emerge and what that change will mean to customers and employees. Along with the vision, the executive needs to describe what values go along with the change and the role that employees will have in making the change work. That vision-values-role description then trickles down to midline and first-line managers. It is their responsibility to interpret the vision for the work unit.

All managers also have to describe, on an ongoing basis, where the organization is in the process of transition. Like a navigator plotting a ship's course on a chart, managers at all levels need to frequently provide information about what has happened recently, what is happening now, and what will happen in the future.

Along with these reports on position, managers have to be prepared to admit their own lack of knowledge or understanding. That, too, is part of the process; team members also have to learn how to cope with incomplete answers or vague descriptions. By modeling their own ability to work with ambiguity, managers can help their team members to muddle through.

The purpose of all this communication is to ensure that employees are aligned with the change. When employees feel they understand why change is taking place, how it will occur, and their role in it, they have taken the first step in the process that will eventually lead them to ownership and acceptance of change.

The risk in these frequent communication reports is that the manager can act as a filter, subtly distorting or reinterpreting information as it trickles from level to level. Another risk is managers acting out their frustration or disagreement with the change process in front of their teams. There can be no surer way to undermine the implementation of change than to do so.

Be accurate. Think through what you are reporting before you say it. How certain are you of your data source?

Tell it like it really is. Provide full disclosure. If things are going well or not going well, employees need to know.

Test the team's understanding. Ask the team to describe how the changes will affect them. If you are conducting a weekly meeting, ask the team to project how current events will affect them this week.

"If you want to build a ship, don't herd people together to collect wood and don't assign them tasks and work, but rather teach them to long for the endless immensity of the sea."
—Antoine de Saint-Exupery

☑ Build new rules for a new game

Your company is becoming more customer oriented and more focused on profitability. To achieve that, certain groups are moving to another state, there is even more automation in order processing, and the sales force is growing. The switch to these new models is going to take six months to a year. Your work unit is in the process of moving and installing new technology, and it looks like a long transition ahead. Meanwhile, this year's goals are as aggressive as they have been in the past. Sound challenging?

This situation calls for an organizational intervention that is unique to change situations. Pretending to operate with yesterday's processes will never work; the answer is for the manager, with the group's help, to develop transition rules for the work unit.

Transition rules are temporary ways of working and communicating that compensate for unusual situations or are designed to preempt problems. Just as the game of golf has winter rules for playing in the off-season, your work unit needs to adopt new temporary policies and procedures for working through the change period.

Forming transition rules takes ingenuity and commitment. Transition rules may ask people to do more work than they would normally do in the new work environment. Or, the tasks may be new or different. Transition rules can affect how work gets done and who does it.

For example, customer orders may have to be double-checked by two different individuals to ensure absolute accuracy, because new automatic editing systems aren't yet available. The whole team may have to come in an hour early during the entire transition process for a daily conference call with internal partners. Or, manual and automatic systems will have to run in parallel with a special team taking responsibility for coordinating the accuracy of information between the two. Or, the manager may ask each team member to practice extra courtesy and patience with other employees to minimize the stress with which people are dealing.

Everyone on the work unit team will be doing a little more than they normally do. Or, they may be asked to do things quite differently. On the other hand, these rules exist to minimize confusion and to ensure accuracy and quality for the customer.

An important part of leading the team through change is developing transition rules. Whether rules involve meetings, work processes, or interpersonal relations, the manager should present the need to the team and discuss how to best deal with the situation.

Explain why transition rules are needed. Transition rules create order where the potential for confusion is great. If the rules are implemented as planned, the team will have a less stressful change experience.

Be there to monitor and enforce the rules. Check whether people are complying with the rules. Find out why rules are working and why they aren't. On the spot, solve problems with implementing rules.

Ask for extra effort. Acknowledge that some of these rules will be a burden to some team members. Ask for their patience and understanding. Emphasize the benefits to everyone in making these rules work.

"Start with good people, lay out the rules, communicate with your employees, motivate them and reward them. If you do all those things effectively, you can't miss."

—Lee Iacocca

☐ ~~Forget the past~~

☑ Remember what is still important

Change can cause crisis in a team. Let's use the example of a downsizing—an especially discomforting change. When reducing the number of workers on the team, the remaining members feel the anxiety and disorientation that major change brings. Some team members may feel uncertain about who will fill the gaps left by former coworkers. Others may feel overwhelmed by the workload and the anxiety that comes from thinking they might be next.

The problem for the team is that important parts of its frame of reference are gone. What used to be a functioning group that had personal relationships, productive experiences, and a routine process are now disparate individuals. They see empty cubicles and offices around them; there are gaping holes in their processes. The reality has shifted to an uneasy place.

The manager of this work unit has to fill that vacuum with not only the vision of the future but also a clear message about what is still relevant and important. What has not changed and probably will not change in the future? When the team understands that, the manager has begun to rebuild the team's frame of reference. The impact is that the environment becomes a little more stable; members may feel the beginnings of a growing sense of control.

What doesn't change? Look for both tangible and intangible facets of your team's work. In the downsizing example, the work product may not change, nor will the quality standards. Certain key players will still be present, sharing their expertise with the team. Most likely, customers will be the same, as will their expectations for quality and performance. Senior management will still be providing direction and support for all work groups in the organization. Positions may shift, but faces will remain the same.

On the intangible side, the mission of the group persists. The group's reputation for performance, insight, quality, effectiveness, or creativity will remain despite the loss of team members. Knowledge about what works and what doesn't— the group's collective wisdom—still remains with the team. The manager's own personal expectations for achieving the group's objectives are still central to the team's experience.

When the manager reinforces these ever-present truths, the team finds itself being drawn back from the confusion of unpredictability and uncertainty. Explaining what has not changed in a convincing, positive way is one of the most important leadership skills that managers need to demonstrate in changing times.

Find the anchors. Think about what priorities still drive the group. On-time delivery of products, quality, ideas, creativity, accuracy, involvement, participation in decision making—these may not be changing at all.

Say it more than once. Use every opportunity to clarify what is still important to the work unit. While the new vision and its benefits are critical for the team to understand, so is what remains.

Create a new frame of reference. Incorporate the vision-values-roles description that change represents into what still exists. Show employees where the past plays a role in the new environment.

"Those who cannot remember the past are condemned to repeat it."

—George Santayana

☐ Stick to policies and procedures

☑ Improvise, adapt, adjust

Imagine you are the manager of a section within the engineering department of a large electronics company. In an effort to reduce cost and boost efficiencies, the entire organization is being asked to integrate and coordinate its activities with other internal partners. For you, that means your work unit will have to work in close alignment with the manufacturing function.

While the idea of breaking down organizational "stovepipes" makes logical sense to you, you and your team have never before really worked collaboratively with other departments. You are not sure how to begin.

The answer is to improvise. Do what makes sense. Start by meeting your counterparts in

Manufacturing; discuss what you mutually need. Ask the team to invent a process of communicating prototype product ideas to Manufacturing, and ask the Manufacturing group to provide feedback. Work on the issues you discover as you proceed. Hold a big off-site meeting and put mental power to work. Or, take small steps, invent, rethink, make up, try out ideas, and learn from them. The process may be easy, or it may be long and challenging.

It is better for your team to figure it out and find its own way than to have a formal, prepackaged solution implanted on it.

Improvisation also plays out on a smaller scale. What if there has been a reorganization in your company, and employees who were considered "back office" operators are now facing customers? How are you going to make this work? Sure, the operators have been given a training program, but what happens in real life? Improvise a system of preparing these people to go on calls: preview their presentations, have rehearsals, send along more experienced salespeople, or debrief their experiences. Do whatever works.

To improvise means to make up solutions without much formal preparation. When you think about it, this can be the fun, opportunity part of change implementation. There may be long sessions where you are striving for consensus, enduring disagreements, and conducting negotiations before what emerges makes sense. Or, the improvised solutions may emerge simply and be put to work. Hopefully, your team will see that the newly invented ways of doing things—after adjustments and improvements—may be more effective than what was done before the change.

Ask the team. Have a meeting, go off-site, and invite internal partners and consultants. If you want the team committed to how things get done, you need to let them design the process.

Keep pressing for a complete solution. Consider what skills people need, new tools that will be helpful, and new measurements or feedback from the manager. Is there a training program that would help? What can you learn from people outside your organization who have faced the same or similar problems?

Document what works. Eventually, what is improvised will become institutionalized. Your team's way can be taught to newcomers as they arrive. In a year or two, it will become "the way we always do it."

"It is not the strongest of the species that survive, nor the most intelligent, but the one most responsive to change."

—Charles Darwin

☐ ~~Take progress for granted~~

☑ Measure and celebrate progress

Gaining commitment to change in the work unit is a challenge all managers face. Change brings uncertainty and may be contradictory to what people believe, value, or assume about how things should be done within an organization. At a certain level, the new vision-values-role that is being espoused by management may be convincing or even desirable to remain competitive and successful in the marketplace. Yet, team members are being asked to commit to an idea whose benefits are only a promise to be achieved sometime in the future.

As a result, it is natural for members of a work unit to be somewhat skeptical about the change being proposed. While people may understand that the change is needed, the belief—and subsequent commitment—that it will work may still be withheld.

One of the most effective ways for managers to fully engage employees in the change process is to demonstrate that the promised results are actually being achieved. For example, if the manager and the team can see that costs are being saved with improved levels of quality and timelier, effective communications, then the change becomes less uncertain.

Will the promised results of change occur all at once, or will they come in small increments? That depends on what the change is. Regardless, the manager should be able to demonstrate improvements in how the team works. Those improvements may be small, anecdotal pieces of evidence that change is taking root or formal measurements of outcomes. The evidence of progress may come from customers, internal partners, upper management, or the team itself.

Movement in the right direction needs to be singled out and celebrated. Consider why this is so important. Team members are making a conscious effort to do things differently. It may require a greater level of effort than ever before on their part, or the change may be pushing individuals far out of their comfort zones.

When team members see progress being made, it does two things. First, progress and improvement validate their personal decisions to give this change a try and muddle through uncomfortable contradictions and ambiguity that change brings. In addition, improvement actually accelerates the adoption of change within the work unit. Success breeds more effort and more success. With change accelerating, the team mostly likely will shed its collective skepticism and begin to believe that this change will actually result in more effective performance. It's up to the manager to highlight those improvements and shout about them.

Find improvements. Look everywhere—work unit processes, outcome measures, and relationships, both internally and with partners and customers. Any improvement counts in a change scenario, especially at the beginning of the process.

Don't wait for perfection. Capture movement in the right direction as work gets done. Remember, it is progress and the effort that that represents that is important in a change situation.

Put progress on the wall. Keep the team informed on a daily basis, if possible, with progress charts and graphs in the work unit's area.

"If there is no struggle, there is no progress."
—Frederick Douglass

☑ Hold the team accountable

People react differently to the idea of change. To some, change represents an opportunity. Initially, these individuals may be somewhat uncertain about what that opportunity is, but they soon engage the change and give it a try. Others are uncomfortable with change in general, and, when a specific work-related change comes their way, these people respond in unproductive ways such as withdrawal, withholding support, or undermining the vision being proposed. A team made up of both these types of individuals may find team performance in jeopardy.

To avoid this scenario, the manager has to make it clear to the work unit that it is ultimately responsible for incorporating new behaviors and procedures into daily activities. While the manager monitors, describes, persuades, provides a role model, and the like, the manager must make it crystal clear that the people doing the work are accountable, as a group, for the progress and success of the implementation.

Toward that end, the manager may assign specific roles to each individual within the team that advance the change in the work unit. For example, an individual may be assigned to ensuring that a new procedure is used in the design of new programs, while another is responsible for checking on how effectively newly designed programs are being implemented in field offices. Another might be asked to try out a new data-gathering instrument to be used with customers. As a whole, the team is responsible for the total implementation.

The manager needs to make this accountability stick by keeping informed of progress and, more specifically, who is doing what. One sure sign that change is going off track is when an individual "forgets" to use a new manual or follow a new procedure, resorting to the old way of doing things. Another is when individuals report they could not implement, say, the new survey because they met some unexpected obstacles put up by another department. Their response was to stop trying.

When these and other signs of team performance drift begin to appear, the manager needs to review with the team what its responsibilities are, what it takes to make change happen (deal with ambiguity, improvise, revisit the vision, and the rest), and reassert expectations for performance.

Depending on his or her unique style, the manager may decide to let the team struggle with the problems it has encountered by itself or step in and get more involved with daily activities.

Accountability means assigning responsibility and holding the team answerable for outcomes. It would be a leadership mistake for the manager to forgive performance slippage or to overlook infractions of transition rules. Change doesn't happen without effort.

Ensure roles are clear. Each team member should know what his or her tasks are and what successful performance looks like.

Monitor implementation. Is the team trying? At what indicators would you look? What happens when obstacles are met? What do team members say about the reasons for success or failure to implement the change?

Expect team effort. Change requires that the team go beyond what it normally does. Let the team know you expect it to work through the difficulties and work out problems, figure out how to adapt, and make progress.

"If everyone is moving forward together, then success takes care of itself."

—Henry Ford

☐ Accept gossip as inevitable

☑ Squash the rumor mill

The most difficult period in changing times is after a change has been announced and before it is finally institutionalized and accepted within an organization. This transition period is called the interim, a special and unusual place between organizational states. A characteristic of this interim period is incomplete or inadequate information. Along with living with contradictory or vague work data or unclear processes, employees may not know with which work units they will merge, who their new manager will be, or whether they will even have the same job, if they have one at all.

The interim period is fertile ground for the generation of rumors. In the tension and suspense of transition, some people find it irresistible to fill in answers to questions with half-truths and large measures of wishful or fantastic thinking. It is human nature to want to consider rumors as valid answers to questions about situations that affect them, even if these explanations are inaccurate or distortions of reality. In change situations, rumors can be a powerful distraction from the important priorities: the implementation, acceleration, and institutionalization of change in a motivated work unit.

A manager can control the rumor mill in several different ways. Probably the easiest way is to ignore the rumors and tell others to do the same. Advise the work unit simply not to listen to rumors when they are presented. A manager can also tell the team to challenge the person transmitting the rumor to substantiate it. Usually, a rumor can't be supported except with the most vague and flimsy reasons.

Some managers actually collect rumors as they ripple through the team and take the time to review them at work unit meetings. Discounting and even ridiculing rumors one by one shows the team how fruitless it is to listen and become preoccupied by them in the first place.

Another way to control rumors is to ask your team not to generate rumors; make this a transition rule. Not passing gossip and rumors about people can be a rule everyone on the team can abide and monitor.

A more active approach is to trace the rumor back to where it came from and deal with the source.

People who frequently generate rumors usually enjoy the impact their rumor makes on others. This person is not doing anyone any favors, especially in a situation that is already filled with tension and insecurity. When the source or sources are discovered, it is time for the manager to have a one-on-one performance discussion with those involved.

Finally, a rumor-filled work unit should be an indicator to the manager that team members are starved for accurate information. This is a sign that management in general needs to increase communications about change throughout the whole organization. Accurate, frequent, and honest information shuts down the rumor mill.

Label rumors when you hear them. Ask people if they know that they are passing along unhelpful gossip.

Explore the implications of rumors. Let your team discuss why rumors can undermine morale and motivation.

Note who seems susceptible to believing rumors. A manager may need to examine why certain individuals feel the need to latch onto rumors in a one-on-one setting.

"The wise speak only of what they know."
—J. R. R. Tolkien

☐ ~~Make decisions by yourself~~

☑ Get team members involved

How would you feel if your manager came into a team meeting and announced that, because of a change in company strategy, a member of the team will have to work on weekends on a rotating basis and that you are going to be expected to come to the office on Saturday at 8 a.m.?

Imagine that your team's structure has changed. Team members will be assigned to field units as their official "ambassador" to headquarters. You are assigned to a work unit in another city without your input or advice. Not too effective, is it?

What is missing is the involvement of team members in making decisions about changes that affect them. Without involvement, resistance is natural. People do not like to feel as if they do not have some level of control of their work lives. On the other hand, management cannot completely delegate change implementation. That would bring a "management by committee" situation, where the team feels it can run the shop as it sees fit. So, how can the manager create involvement that builds commitment and still implement desired and required new directions?

The prudent manager recognizes that when team members contribute to decisions about change, their understanding of the change itself increases, as does their commitment to making change happen. The manager is responsible for defining the boundaries of the involvement. For example, a manager may specify a particular goal that represents an organizational shift. "We are moving to weekend coverage." Then the manager can ask the team for input and ideas on how that can be best implemented. What guidelines are needed? How will the weekend rotation system work? Then the manager can make the decision using input from the group.

Alternatively, if the organization is going to assign "ambassadors" to different field units, the manager may decide to let the team figure out which team member should be assigned to what field unit. The goal is met; the team has created the plan.

Like many change situations, there are strategic decisions that are nonnegotiable. Giving individual managers and their teams the opportunity to design how they will implement these changes goes a long way to imbedding the change. Then again, if there is no choice in the implementation across the organization, then the manager may have the latitude to decide who will be involved on the team. If that is prescribed, then perhaps the manager can decide how the message about change is going to be delivered. Somewhere along the implementation process, managers and teams need to feel they have meaningful ideas, that their input is valued, and that they can contribute to the implementation process.

Involvement breeds familiarity and ownership. Even naysayers and cynics can be turned around if they have a meaningful role in the process of change.

Build in choices. Let the team generate a number of alternative approaches, or present them with a menu of options. Either way, your work unit can come to the consensus about what works best.

Define the boundaries of involvement. Be clear about what the change is, what choices the team has, and what is required.

"Many hands make light work."
—John Heywood

☑ Reward the team for progress

Probably the strongest tool a manager has in his or her toolkit for supporting performance is positive reinforcement. When used in a change situation, positive reinforcement not only acknowledges progress, it also salutes the extraordinary effort the team has made in getting change implemented in the work unit. There are several key ideas to pay attention to when providing rewards to the team.

First, the reward has to be tied directly to a specific achievement, a milestone on the path to implementation, or a final and complete resolution of persistent problems. Although appearing spontaneously one Friday afternoon with pizza for the whole team is surely a welcome and appreciated break from routine, there should be a clear message about what the gesture is for. "I appreciate the effort the team has made this week on moving all the accounts from the old database to the new one by the deadline" can be all the link that is needed.

Most managers think of financial rewards as positive reinforcement. For example, the team receives free tickets to a sporting event; each team member gets a cash payment; the company provides a gift certificate for a shopping spree. A more extreme example is a company "meeting" at a vacation resort or individual travel rewards for each team member. For some people, financial rewards are an appreciated but fleeting gesture; to others, the amount is never enough.

Of course, there are nonfinancial rewards that may have great meaning to the work team. Public recognition, plaques, and certificates may represent achievement or acceptance into a distinguished group of employees. Time off is often a highly valued reward, especially when it is linked to the achievement of a change milestone.

Other nonfinancial rewards may have a more lasting effect. Changing the location of the entire work unit to a more desirable setting might be one. Having visibility and access to higher management may have a positive impact. Finally, the result of the change—fewer delays, more efficient work processes, less stress and frustration, and better customer relationships—are all a direct result of achieving the goals of the change process. That, too, is a potent form of reward.

Rewards make people feel valued and part of a community. Their contributions and team citizenship are acknowledged by all these methods. However, some individuals—whether because of cultural or individual backgrounds—find these forms of acknowledgment to be either personally embarrassing or not especially significant. Before providing rewards, the manager should determine how the recipients will perceive rewards and how they should be presented to individuals.

Regardless of what the rewards are or how they are given, a manager who is leading a team through change needs to ensure the rewards—in whatever form they take—represent sincere and genuine thanks to the team for its achievements and efforts.

Ask the team what rewards it finds valuable. Don't guess; test ideas on team members before investing.

Money isn't always rewarding. Don't assume cash rewards carry the same connotation and value as a more lasting acknowledgment.

Tie rewards to progress. Set a goal, announce the reward for achieving the goal, and deliver the reward immediately upon achievement.

"Winners take time to relish their work, knowing that scaling the mountain is what makes the view from the top so exhilarating."

—Denis Waitley

SHOW A PATH TO INDIVIDUALS:
Help people get unstuck

Despite the best efforts of a change leader to lead a team through, certain individuals will inevitably get stuck. While some people view change as exciting and filled with opportunities, others experience change in different terms—as a threat or a loss.

Whether it's a personal inability to cope with uncertainty and ambiguity or the overwhelming speed of change that immobilizes them, some team members will have a difficult time positively engaging the change situation.

Resistance comes from many sources: confusion about what to do and how to do it, wondering about the future, new role ambiguity, stress from increased work and worry, or lack of information. Even high-performing employees and devoted team members can experience these kinds of individual reactions. Managers can expect to see performance issues emerge from unexpected sources. These performance issues come from the stress of change, not from garden-variety underperformance.

The change leader has to be ready to counsel individuals who are stuck in the transition of change and are unable to move on. Understanding, patience, empathy, positive action, and a sincere and honest forum for dissatisfaction can go a long way toward helping individuals cope.

Show a path to individuals describes actions a change leader can take to help people through change with optimism, encouragement, firmness, reality, and trust.

"Everyone hears only what he understands."
—Goethe

☑ Understand natural reactions to change

From the time a change is announced to when the change takes root, all employees—regardless of level of experience—will go through a certain level of confusion and stress and a sense of loss. What is most interesting about change is that people react to this uncertainty in different ways. Managers who are showing a path to individuals during change need to understand clearly what those individual reactions are.

Some individuals are better able to cope with the disruption of change because they have developed a perspective through their life and work experiences that views change as an opportunity. Initially, these people feel the same disorientation, discomfort, and concern about their futures as do others. But they adapt more quickly, become engaged with the process, tolerate ambiguity, and creatively improvise solutions to new problems. The communications and training programs that usually accompany change initiatives are welcome and sought-after sources of information. This personal, adaptable quality within an organization makes a manager's job easier. Unfortunately, not every employee adapts this way.

Where some employees adapt, others get stuck. Change represents a loss to these other types of people. This loss is usually perceived as greater than whatever gain the change promises. Control, future opportunities, predictability, power, status, security, or many other feelings that are important to this group of people are viewed as changed for the worse or gone.

Other people may put themselves in the role of victim. Victim-employees feel that they have no choice, that they are being "told" what to do, and that their role is to comply.

Another typical reaction is inflexibility and rigidity. This response happens when people become comfortable and habituated with the way things are done, with work processes, and with the form the organization takes. These people neglect to connect how they work with what the purpose of that work is. The importance of the goal and the process are inverted, with the process becoming more significant. When change affects how things are done—new processes, new technologies, new policies—these people react with resistance.

Among other reactions, people who have difficulty coping feel a sense of disenchantment with the organization, longing for the "good old days" and "the way we used to do things." Other behavioral expressions are withdrawal from contributing and a sense of isolation, denial ("This, too, will pass"), and cynicism in formerly engaged employees. Some employees express their resistance by not making decisions or taking action because of imperfect information or incomplete process.

Even excellent performers can get stuck in change. The manager needs to recognize their behavior as a reaction to change and not as a performance issue.

Closely observe behavior. Watch what people say and do in meetings and informal settings. Become sensitive to how people feel.

Study how people react. Learn the underlying psychology of the change experience through courses, texts, and books.

Recognize that these reactions impact everyone. To a greater or lesser degree, all employees react to change. Expect it; look for it.

"Progress is a nice word. But change is its motivator. And change has its enemies."
—Robert Kennedy

☐ Let people figure it out

☑ Customize help for struggling individuals

The manager needs to study how individuals struggle with accepting change so he or she can help them through the transition. There are four broadly defined barriers that individuals may experience. An individual employee may struggle with any or all of these challenges. For each, the manager has to employ a different response.

The first barrier is some form of resistance that may be short-lived or become a chronic issue, depending on the individual. Change, for people stuck here, has a negative connotation, and they find it difficult to see or accept the positive aspects of the change. The role of the manager is to motivate these individuals by defining how the positive aspects of change will impact the individual.

The next barrier is loss of self-control. Some individuals will face obstacles when changes develop in the way work gets done, and, in the confusion and disorientation that follow, their sense of personal control evaporates. What used to be familiar is now distressingly strange. Individuals might find it hard to comprehend new systems and procedures. They struggle to relearn their work, to forge new relationships, or to apply new skills that are required in the new environment. What these employees need is clear, step-by-step coaching and guidance through one-on-one meetings with the manager as well as team discussions. Eventually, these individuals will be better able to handle situations more comfortably.

The third challenge that people struggle with is loss of power. Where an individual formerly had sign-off authority or was able to initiate work and mobilize activity, that individual now has to make decisions as part of a team or with management approval. Or, the work organization has changed so that an individual no longer has the personal connections on which he or she had relied to get things done. This is a difficult area to manage, because individuals often have their personal self-esteem correlated to their level of authority within the organization. Regardless, the manager has to help the individual see what has been gained. Acting as a role model, especially if the manager has experienced a loss of authority, might be helpful, too.

Finally, the challenge may be so formidable that individuals are unable to accept even the most tantalizing benefits. For example, a company is moving to a new location and the individual in question would be promoted to a new job, with new responsibilities and greatly enhanced salary. If that employee's family commitments or professional obligations conflict with that move, accepting the change would be a difficult personal sacrifice. The manager needs to acknowledge the employee's dilemma and respect his or her decision to opt out of the change entirely.

Significant change is never easy. If they can recognize the challenges with which individuals struggle in trying to accept change, managers can help people through the difficulties they face.

Identify challenges in accepting change. People struggle with resistance, loss of control and power, or face difficult personal choices.

Recognize your role. Managers are responsible for helping individuals recognize and manage the challenges they face.

Communicate your intentions. Let your team know you are available and willing to work through the challenges they personally face in working through change.

"Leadership is getting someone to do what they don't want to do to achieve what they want to achieve."

—Tom Landry

☐ ~~Keep your distance~~

☑ Offer empathy

An employee who is having a difficult experience with change is probably working under stress, feels unclear about his or her future career, stays later and comes in earlier, and is generally on edge. What this person needs from his or her manager is empathy. Here's what empathy sounds like:

"I know it's tough coming in early for those conference calls, Kathy. We only have a couple more weeks of that before we go to the new system."

"I understand why you are complaining about the other department, Stan. Not getting the responses we expected can be very frustrating, and you've had more than your share of frustration this week."

"So, reporting to the Executive Committee isn't what you expected, right Gail? I know they have a lot of high standards that can be tough to meet."

What is going on here? Empathy is being used to dissipate and diffuse feelings of frustration, anger, or stress. Notice that the manager in each case is acknowledging the feeling the employee has expressed. In a change situation, there is a lot of emotion and even drama in the workplace. When the manager recognizes this is happening through empathy, he or she is helping individuals in a number of ways.

Acknowledging the emotions that change generates in people makes those high-charged feelings legitimate. The message is that change is stressful and often frustrating, and it is all right and normal to have these feelings. Once expressed, that anger and frustration may begin to abate.

Empathy also opens up communications. Anxiety and uncertainty are not the usual feelings work regularly generates. When these are acknowledged, permission is given, in a way, to talk about these emotions.

Finally, demonstrating empathy sets a tone for the climate of the work unit. The manager is sending a signal that he or she is interested in people, cares about their experience with change, and is willing to listen to their issues, concerns, complaints, and grumblings, however minor or immature sounding. From this simple act, the work unit feels like a friendlier place, even a refuge in a changing organization.

It is important to bear in mind that empathy is acknowledgement, not agreement. It would be a different conversation if the manager took sides with the employee when that person complained about the other department. If that were the case, the employee's anger would probably grow instead of dissipate. In addition, the manager has to be careful that expressions of empathy are not interpreted as agreement. "I know the way you feel" is different from "yes, that department has done nothing to help us, and we have to suffer as a result." Even if that statement were true, it encourages and imbeds resentment rather than diffusing it.

Acknowledge people's feelings. Let people know they have been heard. That recognition helps open up the emotions bottled up by change.

Avoid agreement. To listen and acknowledge is different than to agree. Beware of how empathy comes across.

Learn from others' perspectives. Listening with empathy give you a window on what people in the unit are experiencing. What themes can you detect?

"With the gift of listening comes the gift of healing."

—Catherine de Hueck

☐ Keep emotions out of it

☑ Actively surface dissatisfaction

Your work unit is moving to a new structure. Some employees' jobs will change dramatically; they will have to learn new skills and gain proficiency quickly. Other employees' jobs will actually become narrower in scope; they will be doing fewer things than they had in the past.

The change has caused much discussion and planning in the work unit. You have noticed that two or three individuals who had been first-rate performers are now withdrawn and moody. Each one was not selected for the job that requires new skills. What should you do?

The answer is to get those people to talk about their feelings. Encourage them to tell you what's on their minds. Find out the source of their dissatisfaction. Usually, dissatisfaction stems from seeing only the negatives in a situation, rather than the positives. If that is the case, the manager can reiterate the vision-statement and how that will positively impact each person. However, lots of other factors can trigger dissatisfaction. When you get employees to verbalize what they are experiencing, you can better diagnose what the issue is.

For example, one employee may believe that his or her new role has a lower profile and less chance for advancement than the other job. From your perspective as a manager, you know this is a clear misconception. Apparently, the formal message about this aspect of the change was missed or misconstrued when it was originally delivered. Now you can correct it.

What if you discover that the source of dissatisfaction is a rumor that is taken as truth? Squash the rumor with facts and take the issue off the table.

What if the team member mentions something about the new job or process that is not working, something the individual suffered silently, not wanting to rock the boat? Now you have an opportunity to fix it.

Many employees want to keep a low profile in changing times. Get them to talk; encourage frank and open discussion whenever there is an opportunity. Ask, "How's it going? What do you think of this? What would you do differently?" Not only can you keep in touch with how people are feeling and demonstrate some empathy, you can determine how to best address individuals' concerns.

What's the risk in opening the door to discussing dissatisfaction? You have no idea what to expect. You may have to listen to emotionally laden talk. Frustration, anger, and discontent may gush out. Listen neutrally, nodding your head, empathizing with but not affirming the team member's perspective. You may have to pry information out of reluctant employees. Whatever the case, the simple act of listening often and sincerely can be beneficial to a team member who is dealing with change.

Encourage open and frank discussion. Tell team members you want to hear their genuine views and opinions.

Listen closely. Use active listening when people are expressing themselves. Take notes, nod, and paraphrase what is said. Do not interrupt until the team members have finished their thoughts.

Check in often. Come back again to the team member and ask for an update. Reinforce the positive aspects of change, advise patience, and maintain ongoing, open communications.

"Most of the successful people I've known are the ones who do more listening than talking."
—Bernard M. Baruch

☑ Pinpoint the positives
for individuals

Organizational change is undertaken first and foremost to benefit the ends of the organization. A reorganization, a change in strategy, a move to a new location, investment in new technology, and the like are designed to create competitive advantage. And, when these kinds of changes are communicated, employees often initially see only the positive consequences accruing to the organization and negative consequences falling to themselves. It's a natural and predictable initial response; any organizational change is going to require people in the work unit to change their behavior—many even their values—to some extent. Most people are resistant to change that feels imposed on them.

A wise management team will also have thought through the positive consequences for individuals and work units. Those consequences have to be spelled out in crystal-clear terms with use of tangible examples, and they need to be communicated on a frequent basis through different media.

When a manager finds an individual who is stuck in the transition process, not able to get past the frustration from lack of time, information, or clarity that change brings, the manager can show a path to that team member by finding personal positive consequences. That means painting a customized picture of the future for that individual, building on what that individual cares about.

For example, in a move to expedite and control customer service quality, imagine that a technically oriented work unit has to transfer incoming customer calls to a customer service work unit instead of handling them. A team member feels that his ability to help customers has been cut off; he valued the gratitude he received from thankful customers that he helped. His personal positive consequence that stems from the change may be that he can become a mentor or trainer for the other team, using his experience to build their expertise. Another consequence is that his time is freed for more interesting engineering projects. Or, he can develop his own expertise in an area in which he is interested. Or, he can have more responsibilities. Somewhere there is a benefit; the manager has to find it.

What if the manager can't find the personal positive outcome for an individual? One way to uncover the positives in a situation is to ask the employee. "What do you want to get out of this change?" The team member may see an opportunity that the manager is missing.

One of the greatest tools available to people going through change is a solid, concrete, and tangible view of the future. That vision, specifically tailored to individuals, can be the magnet that pulls people through.

Know your team member's interests and values. A personal positive consequence must link to what an individual finds interesting and important to her or him.

Enthusiasm helps. Accentuating the positive means putting energy and genuine sincerity behind your portrayal of the future. Believe it yourself before you tell others.

Use clear descriptions. No one can guarantee the future. But the more detailed you can paint the positive consequences, the better.

"Perpetual optimism is a force multiplier."
—Colin Powell

☐ ~~Just get the job done~~

☑ Tailor positive tasks for individuals

An individual is stuck in the transition of change. Usually an engaged and talented performer, she feels opportunities for advancement have diminished because of a more team-oriented environment. She feels she no longer can stand out as the "star player" she has been in the past, and she broods about her visibility. To lose her to a competitive organization would be a true loss to the team and the company. What can a manager do?

Research has shown that individual attitudes can be changed through involvement in activities that yield a positive outcome. In this case, the manager and employee can agree on a project that will, say, create a balanced recognition program for team performance. Assigning this individual to work with a group of others ensures that the outcome will be well rounded and meaningful. What does involvement with positive outcomes do to individuals stuck in change?

For one thing, the employee will get to fully explore an issue or task. If the assignment is to build a better way to deal with transferred calls as part of a strategic change, team members will better understand the advantages of different approaches, the constraints that exist, and the reasons why a particular solution is the best, given the circumstances.

Another consequence of involvement is the opportunity to significantly influence and shape how change is implemented. Change in organizations can feel imposed from the top down. Giving team members an assignment to make decisions about how the change is implemented or to improve how the change is working provides choice and control, two important aspects of motivation and engagement.

Finally, with involvement comes acceptance. When a team member who has struggled with change has designed, say, tracking systems that reduce confusion or job aids that boost efficiency, that individual has contributed to a positive outcome. Now, that same individual can communicate and support those ideas to his colleagues. The change has become transferred from something that is being handed down to the team's own approach or accommodation.

Positive actions replace negative thoughts to some extent. Assigning positive tasks and projects to stuck team members may not be a universal remedy in overcoming resistance to change, but it does send a message about optimism, sets up a work climate of participation and choice, and channels energy away from nonproductive responses. The cynic has a useful role to play; the isolated or withdrawn employee gets drawn in, and the team member confused by new roles and relationships gets a chance to clarify and define.

Ask team members to fix what is broken. Look around the work unit at processes, measures, procedures, policies, and staffing. Find what needs to work better, faster, easier, and cheaper.

Match assignments to concerns. If a team member is hung up on procedures, ask him or her for solution ideas. If communication isn't up to standards, assign the task of developing a routine for team communication.

Expect solutions, not redefined problems. Ask for answers, creative ideas, or alternatives that will work to help the work unit. Don't settle for a response that delves into why the change won't work.

"A pessimist sees the difficulty in every opportunity; an optimist sees the opportunity in every difficulty."

—Sir Winston Churchill

☐ ~~Reinforce the good old days~~

☑ Encourage individuals to let go of the past

Ending old ways can be difficult for individuals at all levels of an organization. Habits tend to endure through many attempts of organizational change. When one airline merged with another, the pilots of the acquired airline still used their old company's flight manuals on the new company's airplanes for years after the change. Bankers who work closely with commercial accounts "forget" to bring other team members into the relationship, acting as gate-keepers instead of relationship managers. Veteran employees tell stories to newer recruits about how things were better in the old days, disparaging the changes at hand as "not as good as it used to be."

Some reluctance to give up crusty habits can be expected. On the other hand, clinging to the past can prevent an individual from getting involved with change and moving on. After all, the past was a predictable, certain world where the work was familiar and routine. Work was done with skills that were honed by experience. More important, in that world of the past, an individual felt a sense of control and could point to a track record of personal success and achievements. Reputations were established in a world that is being left behind. If the future looks vastly different, it is natural to expect people to be fearful of what lies ahead.

One way the manager can lead the way into the change is by being clear about expectations. The manager should frequently and clearly describe what the new vision is and the behaviors that are required. "We are going to present specialists in different areas to our clients. That means, as a relationship manager, you have to organize whom to introduce to your best clients, coordinate the specialists' approaches, and bring them up to speed on client needs." The manager can be clear that success now means getting with the program.

Another idea is to symbolically bury the old way. Some managers stage a farewell event in the work unit, taking tangible symbols of the past—letterhead with old logos, product manuals, even pieces of furniture—and tossing them away. Although theatrical, the event marks a punctuation point in the life of the work team. The message is that the past is gone;

it is time to move to the next stage. This time can be the date—the "stake in the ground"—from which the team will measure how far it has come and improved in the future.

Finally, the manager can show a path to stuck individuals by asking them to simply give the new way a try. "Try it; you might like it." Of course, empathy, positive reinforcement of the vision, and sensitivity to why people are struggling helps as well.

Clarify behavioral standards. At some level, change involves new behaviors. Be clear about what those are; contrast and compare them with the old way of doing things.

Manage symbols. Send a message by removing symbols of the past. Get rid of the old signs, logos, and the like. Install new symbols of the future. Hanging on to old representations can confuse people.

Label retro thinking. Don't tolerate too many wasn't-the-past-great discussions or let them go on too long. Saying "that was then; this is now" can bring people back to the present and ready for the future.

"The difficulty lays not so much in developing new ideas as in escaping from old ones."
—John Maynard Keynes

☐ Always ~~endorse~~ the
company line

☑ Stand up for people if they are right

Change is usually carefully designed at the organization level to achieve specific competitive advantage. Opening up new markets, installing technologies and creating new methods, and relocating facilities all have an intended impact on the business. Not every impact of change can be predicted, however. In fact, at the work unit level, affected team members will often be the first to recognize the unintended consequences of change.

For example, a new Web-based order-entry system has instructions that, while present on the site, are somewhat obscure to the normal user. As a result, your customer service work unit is fielding many more calls from confused customers, and there is no end in sight. The impact on individual performance is dramatic. What has been promised as a more efficient vehicle for customer ordering has stressed many team members. The Web designers don't view the issue as that important; neither do their managers.

Should the manager advise his team to figure out a way to adapt to the call volume or bring the issue up with management?

When the change situation is producing unexpected results that impact the customer and have a negative effect on the team, management needs to know. The message has to go straight to the organization's change champion, usually a senior executive responsible for coordinating, designing, and implementing new approaches.

How does this practice help individuals on the team who are having a difficult time dealing with change? It demonstrates that change itself is not perfect, rigid, and immutable. To improve, changes themselves need adjustment and correction. The message is that everyone in the changing organization needs to be flexible, too.

More important, it shows the manager is in touch with what team members are experiencing and is willing to take action—and sometimes take a risk—to fix what is causing problems.

The key is for the manager to know when to stand up. If an individual can demonstrate that unintended consequences are increasing costs, decreasing quality, or negatively impacting the customer, then clearly it is a case to bring up to the hierarchy. But what about an individual who finds he or she is "working harder" or who claims work is "unfairly distributed"? Only gathering and sorting out the facts will reveal whether the individual has a point.

When a manager takes a position to defend an individual's perspective, or even to seriously investigate his or her complaints, the trust between the people involved grows. When trust abounds in a change situation, the future looks less threatening.

Explore complaints. Find out the facts underlying an individual's concern. What is the cause? Who is affected? What's the fix?

Report unintended consequences. Broadcast unforeseen outcomes to all stakeholders involved. Chances are, these results are as surprising to them as they are to you.

Let individuals know you are defending their point of view. Don't hide your efforts; go public when you know you and they are right.

"When you're part of a team, you stand up for your teammates. Your loyalty is to them. You protect them through good and bad, because they'd do the same for you."

—Yogi Berra

"To be a successful leader of change, a manager has to first understand the dynamics of change and how uncertainty affects them and others. The change leader has to recognize how ambiguity can be used to adapt to changes, how improvisation forces work units to make the best of their situations, and how change ratchets up the need for clear, crisp communications."

"Powerful organizational changes contain an underlying loss. Gone is our comfort zone. Gone is the predictability and certainty of the past. We don't know what to expect. We feel at odds with the future; our sense of security goes down. At the root of this sense of loss is fear. That is what makes change so difficult to deal with. People become fearful when certainty goes away."

"The managers of an organization provide the bridge from the old way of doing things to new work practices. Paradoxically, these managers are also employees who experience the same reactions as everyone else."

"The manager needs to paint a picture for the work unit about the hows and whys of change, bringing the messages clearly and honestly to the team. When the task is done well, confusion, stress, and worry about the future is more under control. And the manager becomes identified as a change champion."

"Demonstrating empathy sets a tone for the climate of the work unit. The manager is sending a signal that he or she is interested in people, cares about their experience with change, and is willing to listen to their issues, concerns, complaints, and grumblings. From this simple act, the work unit feels like a friendlier place."

"Resistance comes from many sources: confusion about what to do and how to do it, wondering about the future, new role ambiguity, and stress from increased work, worry, and lack of information. Even high-performing employees and devoted team members can experience these kinds of individual reactions."

"The change leader has to be ready to counsel individuals who are stuck in the transition of change and are unable to move on. Understanding, patience, empathy, positive action, and a sincere and honest forum for dissatisfaction can go a long way toward helping individuals cope."

The McGraw-Hill Mighty Manager's Handbooks

The Powell Principles
by Oren Harari (0-07-144490-4)

Details two dozen mission- and people-based leadership skills that have guided Colin Powell through his nearly half-century of service to the United States.

Provides a straight-to-the-point guide that any leader in any arena can follow for unmitigated success.

How Buffett Does It
by James Pardoe (0-07-144912-4)

Expands on 24 primary ideas Warren Buffett has followed from day one.

Reveals Buffett's stubborn adherence to the time-honored fundamentals of value investing.

The Lombardi Rules
by Vince Lombardi, Jr. (0-07-144489-0)

Presents more than two dozen of the tenets and guidelines Lombardi used to drive him and those around him to unprecedented levels of success.

Packed with proven insights and techniques that are especially valuable in today's turbulent business world.

The Welch Way

by Jeffrey A. Krames (0-07-142953-0)

> Draws on the career of Jack Welch to explain how workers can follow his proven model.

> Shows how to reach new heights in today's wide-open, idea-driven workplace.

The Ghosn Factor

by Miguel Rivas-Micoud (0-07-148595-3)

> Examines the life, works, and words of Carlos Ghosn, CEO of *Nissan* and *Renault*.

> Provides 24 succinct lessons that managers can immediately apply.

How to Motivate Every Employee

by Anne Bruce (0-07-146330-5)

> Provides strategies for infusing your employees with a passion for the work they do.

> Packed with techniques, tips, and suggestions that are proven to motivate in all industries and environments.

The New Manager's Handbook

by Morey Stettner (0-07-146332-1)

> Gives tips for teaming with your employees to achieve extraordinary goals.

> Outlines field-proven techniques to succeed and win the respect of both your employees and your supervisors.

The Sales Success Handbook

by Linda Richardson (0-07-146331-3)

>Shows how to sell customers—not by what you tell them, but by how well you listen to what they have to say.

>Explains how to persuasively position the value you bring to meet the customer's business needs.

How to Plan and Execute Strategy

by Wallace Stettinius, D. Robley Wood, Jr., Jacqueline L. Doyle, and John L. Colley, Jr. (0-07-148437-X)

>Provides 24 practical steps for devising, implementing, and managing market-defining, growth-driving strategies.

>Outlines a field-proven framework that can be followed to strengthen your company's competitive edge.

How to Manage Performance

by Robert Bacal (0-07-148439-8)

>Provides goal-focused, common-sense techniques to stimulate employee productivity in any environment.

>Details how to align employee goals and set performance incentives.

The Handbook for Leaders

by John H. Zenger and Joseph Folkman (0-07-148438-8)

>Identifies 24 competencies essential for becoming an effective and extraordinary leader.

>Provides a systematic program for attaining, developing, and implementing the skills.

About the Author

Michael D. Maginn, Ed.D., is President and CEO of Singularity Group, a leadership, sales, and management consultancy in Hamilton, Massachusetts. He is the author of *Making Teams Work* and *Effective Teamwork*.